Perfecting
the Sounds of
AMERICAN
ENGLISH

Bernard Silverstein, Ph.D.

NTC Publishing Group
a division of NTC/Contemporary Publishing Company

Library of Congress Cataloging-in-Publication Data
Silverstein, Bernard.
        Perfecting the sounds of American English / Bernard Silverstein.
        p. cm.
    ISBN 0-8442-0481-1
    1. English language—United States—Pronunciation. 2. English
language—United States—Pronunciation by foreign speakers. I. Title.
PC2815.S53   1997
421'.52'0973—dc21   96-44515

ISBN: 0-8442-0481-1

Published by National Textbook Company,
a division of NTC/Contemporary Publishing Company,
4255 West Touhy Avenue,
Lincolnwood (Chicago), Illinois 60646-1975 U.S.A.
© 1997 by NTC/Contemporary Publishing Company
7 8 9 V P 0 9 8 7 6 5 4 3 2 1

CONTENTS

INTRODUCTION

Perfecting the Sounds of American English is ideal for native and nonnative speakers of English who would like to improve their ability to speak, spell, and read American English.

Learning to pronounce and spell English words is especially difficult because some sounds of the language can be spelled in many different ways. For example, the vowel sound in the word *eat*, represented by the phonetic symbol [i], can be spelled thirteen different ways, as illustrated in the following English words: C*ae*sar, b*e*, s*ea*, b*ee*, rec*ei*ve, L*eigh*, k*ey*, safar*i*, bel*ie*f, subp*oe*na, q*uay*, mosq*ui*to and funn*y*. Pronunciation is especially difficult to learn because the correct pronunciation for each word often must be memorized, rather than determined by the way it is spelled.

This guide instructs the reader in the use of phonetic symbols, how to produce the sounds that go with them, and the way the sounds are used in English. To learn the IPA symbols, the user can enlist the services of a volunteer model speaker or use a prerecorded audiocassette made for this book. The model speaker should be an American English speaker with good, clear pronunciation. Instructions for serving as a model speaker are provided. This guide is designed to help the user learn the correct perception and production for all the vowel, diphthong, and triphthong sounds of American English as well as the consonant sounds and consonant blends.

In addition, the material helps the user process the sounds in words better and to remember the sounds in their proper sequence. Information on speech syllabification and syllable stress improves both the comprehension and production of American English speech.

This guide makes American English pronunciation easy to learn, by using a simplified version of the International Phonetic Alphabet (IPA) in which each sound of the language is represented by one phonetic symbol. This book has been compiled to meet the special needs of a number of different groups.

1. Students of English as a Second Language, in the United States and throughout the world, who wish to improve their articulation, pronunciation, reading, and spelling skills.

2. Nonnative speakers of English who are teachers of English as a Second Language who wish to improve their articulation, pronunciation, syllabification, and syllable stress.

3. Native speakers of American English who wish to acquire a General American English pronunciation.

4. Persons with significantly defective speech sound production who wish to improve articulation and pronunciation skills.

5. Persons with hearing impairment who wish to learn how to produce the speech sounds of English and how to pronounce a large vocabulary.

6. Persons who wish to learn how to read English, or improve their reading and spelling skills and increase their vocabulary.

7. Students of phonetics who wish to learn to read and write broad phonetic transcription using the International Phonetic Alphabet and learn speech syllabification and syllable stress.

8. Professional speakers, students of radio or television broadcasting, and singers who wish to have a pronunciation reference guide and material for improving their articulation and pronunciation skills.

9. Teachers of English as a Second Language, audiologists and speech-language pathologists, teachers of the hearing impaired, reading specialists, teachers of reading, and teachers of phonetics.

OUR QUEER LANGUAGE

When the English tongue we speak,
Why is "break" [brek] not rhymed with "freak" [frik]?
Will you tell me why it's true
We say "sew" [so] but likewise "few" [fju];
And the maker of a verse
Cannot cap his "horse" [hɔɚs] with "worse" [wɚs] ?
"Beard" [bɪɚd] sounds not the same as "heard" [hɚd];
"Cord" [kɔɚd] is different from "word" [wɚd];
Cow is "cow" [kæʊ] but low is "low"[lo];
"Shoe" [ʃu] is never rhymed with "foe" [fo].
Think of "hose" [hoz] and "dose" [dos] and "lose" [luz];
And think of "goose" [gus] and yet of "choose" [tʃuz].
Think of "comb" [kom] and "tomb" [tum] and "bomb" [bɑm];
"Doll" [dɑl] and "roll" [rol] and "home" [hom] and "some" [səm];
And since "pay" [pe] is rhymed with "say" [se];
Why not "paid" [ped] with "said" [sɛd], I pray?
We have "blood" [bləd] and "food" [fud] and "good" [gʊd];
"Mould" [mold] is not pronounced like "could" [kʊd].
Wherefore "done" [dən] but "gone" [gɔn] and "lone" [lon]?
Is there any reason known?
And, in short, it seems to me
Sounds and letters disagree.

(*Author unknown*)
Phonetic transcriptions have been
added to the original poem

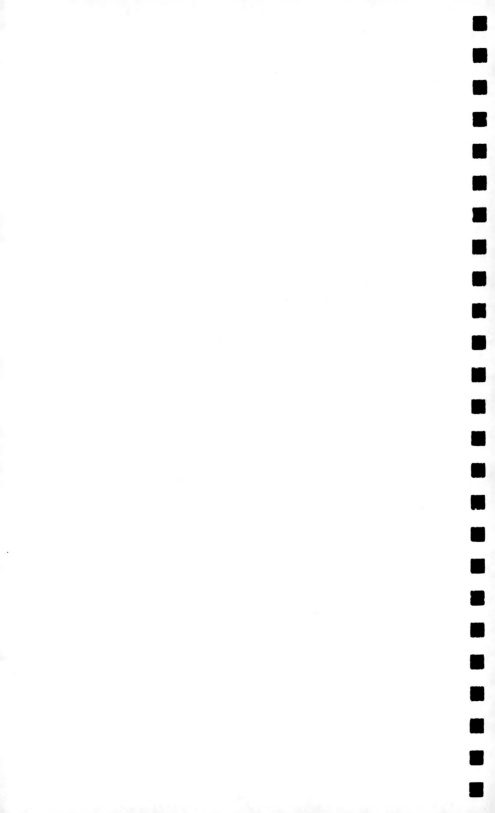

PRONUNCIATION GUIDE

Notes on the Tables

Refer to Tables 1–9 on pages P-5 through P-13.

Table 1 The Vowel and Diphthong Sounds of American English

Column 1 contains the I.D. number for each of the vowel sounds of American English and the vowel combinations for the three phonemic diphthongs. The same numbers are found in Table 2.

Column 2 contains the I.P.A. vowel symbols for the vowel and diphthong sounds used throughout this guide. It is a simplified set of symbols representing all the vowel and diphthong sounds used in General American English, except those made with [l] and [r].

Column 3 contains the most typical spelling for each of the vowel and diphthong sounds. Alternative common spelling equivalents are also indicated in the basic information provided with the practice lists for each of the sounds.

Columns 4, 5, and 6 contain common, frequently used illustrative words for each sound in the initial, medial, and final positions in words. A dash (—) is used to indicate that a sound does not occur in one or more of these positions in American English.

Table 2 American English Vowel Sound Production

Table 2 contains information about how the twelve vowel sounds are produced. Each sound has its own vowel quality based on where in the mouth it is produced. For example, the vowel sounds 1–5 are all produced in the front of the mouth. But as Table 2 indicates, the position of the tongue is pulled back somewhat as the tongue is lowered slightly for some and more for others.

This information is also found in the basic information provided for each sound, which accompanies the word lists for each vowel sound. Table 2 does not provide information on the presence or absence of tongue tension, which modifies the texture of the mouth cavity and helps determine the vowel quality.

Lowering the position of the tongue within the oral cavity is made possible by increasing the mouth opening by lowering the jaw.

The degree of mouth opening along with the shape of the lips determines the visible components of the vowel and diphthong sounds.

Table 3 The Vowels [l] and [ɚ] Diphthong and Triphthong Sounds of American English

Column 1 contains the I.D. numbers for the vowel and diphthong sounds that combine with the vowel [l] and [ɚ] sounds to produce diphthongs and triphthongs. Column 2 contains the I.P.A. phonetic symbols for the sounds. Columns 3, 4, and 5 contain commonly used illustrative words for each diphthong and triphthong in the initial, medial, and final positions. A dash is used to indicate that the combination does not occur in a particular position.

Table 4 The Consonant Sounds of American English

Column 1 contains the I.D. numbers for the consonant sounds. The sequence of numbers is based on the alphabetical order of the typical spelling equivalents listed in column 3.

Column 2 contains the I.P.A. phonetic symbols for the consonant sounds. Columns 4, 5, and 6 contain commonly used illustrative words for each consonant sound in the initial, medial, and final positions. A dash is used to indicate that the sound does not occur in a particular position.

Table 5 American English Consonant Sound Production

Table 5 contains classification information for the consonant sounds. The table organizes the sounds by similarities and differences in their production and helps to explain why they sound the way they do. In classifying a sound the voicing information is usually mentioned first, followed by the place of articulation and then the manner of production. For example, the [p] sound is referred to as a "voiceless, bilabial, stop-plosive" and the [ʃ] sound is a "voiceless, alveolar-palatal, fricative." Descriptive information about the five manners of production may be found on pages P-26, 27.

It should be noted that the two affricate sounds [tʃ] and [dʒ] are combinations of two sounds that have different places of articulation. To produce these sounds the tongue moves back from the alveolar ridge to the area of the hard palate.

Table 6 Final Sounds for Plural Nouns in American English

This table indicates how nouns are normally pluralized depending on the final sound of the noun. The Table does not include the consonant sounds [h], [l], [r], [w], [ʍ], [j] because these sounds either do not occur in the final position of words or are considered to be vowel sounds in the final position.

There are a few exceptions to the rules of pluralizing words such as the words *foot* and *feet*, *tooth* and *teeth*, *man* and *men*, *woman* and *women*, *life* and *lives* etc. This guide does not normally include regular plural nouns, but does include third person singular, present tense verbs which are spelled and pronounced the same as the plural nouns.

Table 7 Final Sounds for Past and Present Tense Verbs in American English

This table indicates how verbs are normally changed to the past tense or third person singular, present tense depending on the final sound of the root word.

Column 2 indicates if the final sound of the root verb is voiced (V) or voiceless (Vs) and column 3 provides a list of illustrative words that are changed to the past tense in column 4 and the third person singular present tense in Column 5. The pronunciations of these tense endings are presented in phonetic transcription in the last column.

Table 8 Consonant Blends in the Initial Position in Words in American English

This table provides a list of illustrative words for the various [l] [r] [s] and [w] blends or clusters that occur in the initial position of words. The lists are in an alphabetical order based on the spelling equivalents of the consonant sounds that produce the blends.

Table 9 Consonant and Vowel [l] and [ɚ] Clusters in the Final Position in Words in American English

Columns 1 and 2 provide lists of words for the vowel [l] and vowel [ɚ] sounds preceded by various consonant sounds listed in alphabetical order of the spelling equivalents. It should be noted that no vowel sound is produced between the consonant and the vowel [l] or vowel [ɚ].

Columns 3 and 4 provide lists of words in which the vowel [l] and vowel [ɚ] sounds are followed by various consonant sounds listed in alphabetical order.

Table 1. **The Vowel and Diphthong Sounds of American English**

I.D. Numbers	Phonetic Symbol	Typical Spelling	Initial Position	Medial Position	Final Position
V-1	[i]	ee	eat	beat	see
V-2	[ɪ]	i	it	bit	—
V-3	[e]	ay	ate	bait	say
V-4	[ɛ]	e	edge	bet	—
V-5	[æ]	a	at	bat	—
V-6	[ɚ]	er	earn	burn	her
V-7	[ə]	u	up	but	sofa
V-8	[u]	oo	ooze	boot	two
V-9	[ʊ]	ou	—	book	—
V-10	[o]	o	okay	boat	sew
V-11	[ɔ]	aw	ought	bought	saw
V-12	[ɑ]	ah	opera	bottle	spa
D-12+2	[ɑɪ]	igh	ice	bite	high
D-5+9	[æʊ]	ow	out	bout	cow
D-11+2	[ɔɪ]	oy	oyster	boys	toy

Table 2. American English Vowel Sound Production

Place of Articulation in the Oral Cavity

Height of Tongue	Front Vowels	Central Vowels	Back Vowels	Degree of Mouth Opening
High Low-High	1 [i] 2[ɪ]		8 [u] 9[ʊ]	Narrow
Mid Low-Mid	3[e] 4 [ɛ]	6 [ɚ] 7 [ə]	10 [o]	Medium
Low Low-Low	5 [æ]		11 [ɔ] 12 [ɑ]	Wide

Table 3. The Vowel [l] and [ɚ] Diphthong and Triphthong Sounds of American English

I.D.	Symbol	Initial	Medial	Final
D-1+l	[il]	eel	peels	peel
D-2+l	[ɪl]	ill	pills	pill
D-3+l	[el]	ale	fails	fail
D-4+l	[ɛl]	else	sells	sell
D-5+l	[æl]	alto	pals	pal
D-6+l	[ɚl]	earl	pearls	pearl
D-7+l	[əl]	ultra	pulse	mull
D-8+l	[ul]	—	pools	pool
D-9+l	[ʊl]	—	pulls	pull
D-10+l	[ol]	old	poles	pole
D-11+l	[ɔl]	all	falls	fall
D-12+l	[ɑl]	olive	dolls	doll
T-12,2+l	[ɑɪl]	I'll	piles	pile
T-5,9+l	[æʊl]	owl	owls	towel
T-11,2+l	[ɔɪl]	oil	boils	boil
D-2+6	[ɪɚ]	ear	clearing	fear
D-3+6	[eɚ]	—	players	mayor
D-4+6	[ɛɚ]	air	pairs	fair
D-5+6	[æɚ]	arrow	carry	—
D-8+6	[uɚ]	—	sewers	bluer
D-9+6	[ʊɚ]	—	touring	sure
D-10+6	[oɚ]	—	mowers	slower
D-11+6	[ɔɚ]	or	boring	four
D-12+6	[ɑɚ]	arch	farther	far
T-12,2+6	[ɑɪɚ]	iron	tires	fire
T-5,9+6	[æʊɚ]	our	showers	sour
T-11,2+6	[ɔɪɚ]	—	foyers	foyer

Table 4. The Consonant Sounds of American English

I.D.	Symbol	Spelling	Initial	Medial	Final
C-1	[b]	b	bow	table	rub
C-2	[tʃ]	ch	choke	teacher	watch
C-3	[d]	d	doe	ready	bed
C-4	[f]	f	foe	before	off
C-5	[g]	g	go	begin	dog
C-6	[h]	h	hoe	behind	—
C-7	[dʒ]	j	joke	danger	page
C-8	[k]	k	coat	because	book
C-9	[l]	l	low	only	—
C-10	[m]	m	mow	summer	home
C-11	[n]	n	no	funny	done
C-12	[ŋ]	ng	—	singer	ring
C-13	[p]	p	poke	happy	cup
C-14	[r]	r	row	around	—
C-15	[s]	s	so	also	face
C-16	[ʃ]	sh	show	washing	wish
C-17	[t]	t	toe	better	eat
C-18	[θ]	th	throw	nothing	mouth
C-19	[ð]	th	though	father	bathe
C-20	[v]	v	vote	over	give
C-21	[w]	w	woe	away	—
C-22	[ʍ]	wh	which	anywhere	—
C-23	[j]	y	yoke	million	—
C-24	[z]	z	zone	busy	his
C-25	[ʒ]	zh	genre	measure	garage

Table 5. American English Consonant Sound Production

Manner of Formation and Voicing

Place of Articulation	Stop-Plosive		Fricative		Affricate		Nasal	Glide
	Vs	V	Vs	V	Vs	V	V	V
Bilabial	[p] 13	[b] 1	wh [ʍ] 22				[m] 10	[w] 21
Labio-dental			[f] 4	[v] 20				
Inter-dental			th [θ] 18	th [ð] 19				
Alveolar	[t] 17	[d] 3	[s] 15	[z] 24			[n] 11	[l] 9
Alveolar-palatal			sh [ʃ] 16	zh [ʒ] 25	ch [tʃ] 2	j [dʒ] 7		y [r] [j] 14 23
Velar	[k] 8	[g] 5					ng [ŋ] 12	
Glottal			[h] 6					

[ ]   = International Phonetic Alphabet Symbol for Sound
V   = Voiced (produced with vocal fold vibration)
Vs   = Voiceless (produced without vocal fold vibration)
Number = in Alphabetical Order of Spelling Equivalent

Bilabial (both lips)
Labio-dental (lower lip and upper front teeth)
Inter-dental (tongue tip between the front teeth)
Alveolar (gum ridge, behind the upper front teeth)
Alveolar-Palatal (gum ridge and hard palate, or just hard palate)
Velar (back of tongue to front of soft palate)
Glottal (between the vocal folds)

Table 6. **Final Sounds for Plural Nouns in American English**

Final Sound of Root Words	Voiced (V) or Voiceless (Vs) Final Sound	Example Words	Plural Words	Plural Endings
[b]	V	cab	cabs	[bz]
[tʃ]	Vs	match	matches	[tʃ ɪz]
[d]	V	bed	beds	[dz]
[f]	Vs	safe	safes	[fs]
[g]	V	bug	bugs	[gz]
[dʒ]	V	cage	cages	[dʒ ɪz]
[k]	Vs	book	books	[ks]
[m]	V	name	names	[mz]
[n]	V	ton	tons	[nz]
[ŋ]	V	ring	rings	[ŋz]
[p]	Vs	cup	cups	[ps]
[s]	Vs	house	houses	[s ɪz]
[ʃ]	Vs	dish	dishes	[ʃ ɪz]
[t]	Vs	cat	cats	[ts]
[θ]	Vs	bath	baths	[θs]
[ð]	V	lathe	lathes	[ðz]
[v]	V	stove	stoves	[vz]
[z]	V	nose	noses	[z ɪz]
[ʒ]	V	corsage	corsages	[ʒ ɪz]

As indicated above, nouns which end in voiced (V) consonant sounds are pluralized by adding a [z] sound to the root word. Nouns ending in a voiceless (vs) consonant are pluralized by adding an [s] sound to the root word. The exceptions to these rules are root words that end in the [tʃ], [dʒ], [s], [z], [ʃ] or [ʒ] sounds, since [s] or [z] plural endings would be difficult to say or hear, and therefore an additional syllable [ɪz] is produced following the final sound of the root word.

Since all vowel, diphthong, and triphthong sounds are voiced, nouns which end in these sounds are pluralized by adding a [z] sound to the root word.

Table 7. Final Sounds for Past and Present Tense Verbs in American English

Final Sound of Root Word	Voiced (V) or Voiceless (Vs) Final Sound	Example Words	Past Tense	Present Tense	Tense Endings
[b]	V	rob	robbed	robs	[bd, bz]
[tʃ]	Vs	reach	reached	reaches	[tʃt, tʃ ɪz]
[d]	V	need	needed	needs	[d ɪd, dz]
[f]	Vs	cough	coughed	coughs	[ft, fs]
[g]	V	beg	begged	begs	[gd, gz]
[dʒ]	V	judge	judged	judges	[dʒd, dʒ ɪz]
[k]	Vs	like	liked	likes	[kt, ks]
[m]	V	climb	climbed	climbs	[md, mz]
[n]	V	fan	fanned	fans	[nd, nz]
[ŋ]	V	long	longed	longs	[ŋd, ŋz]
[p]	Vs	help	helped	helps	[pt, ps]
[s]	Vs	miss	missed	misses	[st, s ɪz]
[ʃ]	Vs	push	pushed	pushes	[ʃt, ʃ ɪz]
[t]	Vs	want	wanted	wants	[t ɪd, ts]
[ð]	V	bathe	bathed	bathes	[ðd, ðz]
[v]	V	move	moved	moves	[vd, vz]
[z]	V	use	used	uses	[zd, z ɪz]
[ʒ]	V	rouge	rouged	rouges	[ʒd, ʒ ɪz]

As indicated above, verbs that end in voiced (V) consonant sounds will have a past tense ending of [d] added to the root verb. Verbs that end in voiceless (Vs) consonants will have a past tense ending of [t] added to the root word. The exception to these rules are root words that end in [d] or [t] when an additional syllable [ɪd] is produced following the root word. Present tense endings for third person singular verbs ending in voiced (v) consonants will have a [z] sound added. Words ending in a voiceless (vs) sound will have an [s] sound added. The exceptions for these rules are for verbs ending in [tʃ], [dʒ], [s], [z], [ʃ] or [ʒ], when an additional syllable [ɪz] is produced following the final sound of the root word.

Since all vowel, diphthong, and triphthong sounds are voiced, all verbs that end in these sounds will have a past tense ending of [d] and a present tense ending of [z] for third person singular words.

Table 8. Consonant Blends in the Initial Position of Words in American English

[l] Blends	[r] Blends	[s] Blends	[w] Blends
[bl] blue	[br] brown	[sk] skin	[dw] dwell
[fl] flag	[dr] drive	[sl] sleep	[kw] quit
[gl] glass	[fr] fresh	[sm] small	[sw] swim
[kl] clock	[gr] green	[sn] snow	[tw] twin
[pl] plate	[kr] crack	[sp] spell	
[sl] slip	[pr] proud	[st] stop	
[spl] split	[ʃr] shrimp	[sw] sweet	
	[tr] trip	[spl] splash	
	[θr] throw	[spr] spray	
	[skr] scream	[str] strong	
	[spr] spring		
	[str] street		

Table 9. Consonant and Vowel [l] and [ɚ] Clusters in the Final Position in Words in American English

Consonant plus Vowel [l] Clusters	Consonant Plus [ɚ] Clusters	Vowel [l] Plus Consonant Clusters	Vowel [ɚ] Plus Consonant Clusters
[bl] bubble	[bɚ] number	[lb] bulb	[ɚb] curb
[dl] ladle	[dɚ] ladder	[ld] build	[ɚtʃ] church
[tʃl] satchel	[tʃɚ] butcher	[lf] gulf	[ɚd] heard
[fl] waffle	[fɚ] wafer	[lk] bulk	[ɚf] surf
[gl] giggle	[gɚ] anger	[lm] film	[ɚdʒ] purge
[kl] wrinkle	[kɚ] broker	[lp] help	[ɚk] turk
[ml] camel	[mɚ] armor	[ls] pulse	[ɚl] pearl
[nl] funnel	[nɚ] corner	[lt] built	[ɚm] germ
[pl] people	[pɚ] paper	[lz] pulls	[ɚn] turn
[sl] whistle	[sɚ] answer		[ɚp] burp
[ʃl] bushel	[ʃɚ] censure		[ɚs] purse
[tl] little	[tɚ] actor		[ɚt] hurt
[θl] brothel	[θɚ] ether		[ɚθ] dearth
[zl] puzzle	[ðɚ] either		[ɚv] curve
	[zɚ] miser		

THE VOWEL, DIPHTHONG, AND TRIPHTHONG SOUNDS OF AMERICAN ENGLISH

PRODUCTION

All vowel sounds are produced with vocal fold vibration, which results when air is pushed from the lungs and passes between the two vocal folds (located in the larynx) that have been brought together, but not closed tightly. As the vowel sounds are produced, this vibration can be felt by placing the thumb and index finger on the front of the neck where the "voice box" is located.

Vocal fold vibration, or "voicing" as it is sometimes called, creates a complex sound that can be modified by changes in the size, shape, or texture of the mouth cavity. The mouth functions as a resonator that selectively changes the laryngeal sound to produce the different vowel sounds of the language.

Table 2, page P-6 contains information for each of the twelve American English vowel sounds, explaining how each of the sounds is produced. The position of the entire tongue plays a major role in producing the different vowel sounds. The tongue can be moved along two dimensions in the mouth, higher or lower and more front or more back. The front vowels, [i] [ɪ] [e] [ɛ] [æ], which are numbered 1 through 5, are made with the tongue more toward the front of the mouth, with the front of the tongue at its highest for [i] and its lowest for [æ]. The central vowels, [ɚ] [ə], which are numbered 6 through 7, are made with the tongue midway between high and low and midway between front and back. The back vowels, [u] [ʊ] [o] [ɔ] [ɑ], which are numbered 8 through 12, are made with the tongue more toward the back of the mouth, with the back of the tongue at its highest for [u] and its lowest for [ɑ]. Some degree of lip rounding accompanies the higher back vowels and [ɚ]. A greater degree of tongue muscle tension in the pronunciation of [i] [e] [u] [o] [ɔ] tends to lengthen these vowels slightly.

When attempting to imitate American English sounds, you should listen very carefully to a model speaker and try to match the sounds you hear by varying the position of the tongue and the size of the mouth cavity, and by changing the lip shape or the muscular tension of the articulators.

Diphthongs, e.g., [ɑɪ] [æʊ] [ɔɪ], are two vowel sounds produced in a sequence with articulators moving from the position of one vowel to the other. Triphthongs, e.g., [ɑɪl] [æʊl] [ɔɪl], and [ɑɪɚ], [æʊɚ], [ɔɪɚ] are three vowel sounds produced in sequence, with the articulators moving from the position of the first vowel, through the position of the second vowel, and reaching the position of the third vowel.

Additional specific information about each vowel and diphthong sound of the language will be found with the word lists for each sound.

THE VOWEL, DIPHTHONG, AND TRIPHTHONG SOUNDS OF AMERICAN ENGLISH

PRONUNCIATION

The following exercises utilize the pronunciation of a native speaker of American English as a model. You can use either the audiocassette available for use with this book or the services of the American English speaker who will read the lists of sounds and words in the tables that follow. The model speaker should pronounce the lists of words clearly and *naturally*. The speaker should *not* pronounce each syllable separately and should not emphasize any syllable that is not normally emphasized. Normal and natural American English is the goal.

First, turn to Table 1 on page P-5. Column 2 contains the IPA symbol for each of the vowel sounds and the diphthong sounds of English (except those that involve the vowel [l] or [ɚ]). Please note in column 1 the identification number for each vowel (V) and diphthong (D) sound.

Please listen to side A of the audiocassette or ask your model speaker to read from the columns as instructed below.

OBJECTIVE 1. To learn the phonetic symbol and identification number for each of the vowel and diphthong sounds.

Procedures:

A. As the model speaker says each sound, listen carefully and point to its phonetic symbol in column 2. Play the tape or ask an English speaker to pronounce the sounds in column 2 in order. (The speaker can identify the correct sound by saying first the example words in columns 4, 5, and 6.)

B. As the model speaker says each sound, write the correct phonetic symbols and I.D. number.
Repeat this procedure until you feel comfortable with the symbols.

OBJECTIVE 2. To be able to identify the vowel and diphthong symbols when they are presented in random order.

Procedures:

A. As the model speaker says the sounds in column 2 in random order, listen carefully and point to the proper symbols. Play the tape or ask an English speaker to pronounce the sounds in column 2 in random order.

B. The model speaker on the audiotape will identify the correct symbol by saying the I.D. number. The English speaker can simply point to the correct symbol.

OBJECTIVE 3. To be able to listen to two vowel or diphthong sounds and decide if the same sound was heard twice or if different sounds were heard.

Procedures:
A. Listen to paired sounds. B. Decide I.D. numbers of sounds heard. C. Listen for correct I.D. numbers. D. Repeat as necessary. (Use the audiotape or a model speaker.)

OBJECTIVE 4. To learn to say each vowel and diphthong sound correctly.

Procedures:
A. Listen to the sound. B. Imitate sound out loud. C. Point to its phonetic symbol. D. Write symbol. E. Listen for correct I.D. number. F. Repeat as necessary. (Use the audiotape or a model speaker.)

OBJECTIVE 5. To learn to identify the diphthong and triphthong sounds involving the vowel [l] and vowel [ɚ] and their phonetic transcriptions.

Procedures:
A. Turn to Table 3. B. Listen to combination of sounds. C. Point to their phonetic symbols. D. Imitate the sound out loud. E. Write the phonetic symbols. F. Listen to the correct I.D. number. G. Repeat as often as necessary. (Use the audiotape or a model speaker.)

OBJECTIVE 6. To listen to the correct production of word lists for each of the vowel and diphthong sounds of American English in the various word positions in which they occur. To learn how to read the phonetic transcriptions of the words and to say them with correct pronunciation.

Procedures:
A. Turn to page P-18 for the word lists for vowel [i]. B. Listen to words with the [i] sound in the initial position. C. Imitate the words heard while looking at the phonetic transcription. D. Continue with word lists for other positions and those with contrasting sounds. E. Continue with the word lists for the other vowel and diphthong sounds. F. Repeat as often as necessary. (Use the audiotape or a model speaker.)

[i]

1. Phonetic symbol and I.D. number: [i], V-1
2. Production information: a high, front, tense vowel
3. Positions in words: initial, medial, and final
4. Typical spellings: sh**e**, s**ea**, s**ee**
5. Visible information: narrow mouth opening, lips spread

[i] Word List

Initial	Medial	Final
east [ist]	keep [kip]	me [mi]
equal ['i kwəl]	need [nid]	free [fri]
even ['i vn]	please [pliz]	key [ki]
eagle ['i gl]	mean [min]	tea [ti]
eager ['i gɚ]	these [ðiz]	she [ʃi]

Contrasting Vowels:

[i]		[ɪ]		[i]		[ɛ]
each [itʃ]	—	itch [ɪtʃ]		feed [fid]	—	fed [fɛd]
eat [it]	—	it [ɪt]		speed [spid]	—	sped [spɛd]
green [grin]	—	grin [grɪn]		deed [did]	—	dead [dɛd]
feel [fil]	—	fill [fɪl]		lease [lis]	—	less [lɛs]
least [list]	—	list [lɪst]		bleed [blid]	—	bled [blɛd]

---

1. Phonetic symbol and I.D. number: [ɪ], V-2
2. Production information: a low-high, front, lax vowel
3. Positions in words: initial and medial
4. Typical spelling: sh**i**p
5. Visible information: narrow mouth opening, lips relaxed

[ɪ] Word List

Initial	Medial
inch [ɪntʃ]	big [bɪg]
ink [ɪŋk]	give [gɪv]
is [ɪz]	him [hɪm]
in [ɪn]	built [bɪlt]
if [ɪf]	city ['sɪt i]

Contrasting Vowels:

[ɪ]		[i]		[ɪ]		[ɛ]
hill [hɪl]	—	heel [hil]		hid [hɪd]	—	head [hɛd]
fit [fɪt]	—	feet [fit]		sit [sɪt]	—	set [sɛt]
sin [sɪn]	—	seen [sin]		lid [lɪd]	—	led [lɛd]
dip [dɪp]	—	deep [dip]		pin [pɪn]	—	pen [pɛn]
ill [ɪl]	—	eel [il]		pig [pɪg]	—	peg [pɛg]

[e]

1. Phonetic symbol and I.D. number: [e], V-3
2. Production information: a mid, front, tense vowel
3. Positions in words: initial, medial, and final
4. Typical spellings: ate, aid, way
5. Visible information: medium mouth opening, with the lips spread, often followed by a narrow-relaxed movement

[e] Word List

Initial	Medial	Final
eight [et]	name [nem]	pay [pe]
ace [es]	rain [ren]	day [de]
acre ['e kɚ]	same [sem]	they [ðe]
ache [ek]	great [gret]	stay [ste]
aim [em]	cake [kek]	play [ple]

Contrasting Vowels:

[e]		[ɛ]		[e]		[æ]
age [edʒ]	—	edge [ɛdʒ]		made [med]	—	mad [mæd]
sale [sel]	—	sell [sɛl]		plane [plen]	—	plan [plæn]
wait [wet]	—	wet [wɛt]		aid [ed]	—	add [æd]
date [det]	—	debt [dɛt]		baked [bekt]	—	backed [bækt]
raid [red]	—	red [rɛd]		lame [lem]	—	lamb [læm]

[ɛ]

1. Phonetic symbol and I.D. number: [ɛ], V-4
2. Production information: a low-mid, front, lax vowel
3. Positions in words: initial and medial
4. Typical spelling: bed
5. Visible information: medium mouth opening, lips spread

[ɛ] Word List

Initial	Medial
else [ɛls]	help [hɛlp]
etch [ɛtʃ]	said [sɛd]
egg [ɛg]	neck [nɛk]
any ['ɛn i]	guess [gɛs]
enter ['ɛn tɚ]	men [mɛn]

Contrasting Vowels:

[ɛ]		[æ]		[ɛ]		[ə]
end [ɛnd]	—	and [ænd]		pep [pɛp]	—	pup [pəp]
leg [lɛg]	—	lag [læg]		fled [flɛd]	—	flood [fləd]
pen [pɛn]	—	pan [pæn]		deck [dɛk]	—	duck [dək]
send [sɛnd]	—	sand [sænd]		ten [tɛn]	—	ton [tən]
then [ðɛn]	—	than [ðæn]		net [nɛt]	—	nut [nət]

[æ]

1. Phonetic symbol and I.D. number: [æ], V-5
2. Production information: a low, front, lax vowel
3. Positions in words: initial and medial
4. Typical spelling: s**a**d
5. Visible information: wide mouth opening, lips spread

[æ] Word List

Initial	*Medial*
at [æt]	map [mæp]
ask [æsk]	has [hæz]
am [æm]	bag [bæg]
add [æd]	had [hæd]
as [æz]	that [ðæt]

Contrasting Vowels:

[æ]	[ɑ]		[æ]	[ə]
sad [sæd]	— sod [sɑd]		pat [pæt]	— putt [pət]
hat [hæt]	— hot [hɑt]		mad [mæd]	— mud [məd]
map [mæp]	— mop [mɑp]		lack [læk]	— luck [lək]
cat [kæt]	— cot [kɑt]		bad [bæd]	— bud [bəd]
pad [pæd]	— pod [pɑd]		bat [bæt]	— but [bət]

---

1. Phonetic symbol and I.D. number: [ɚ], V-6
2. Production information: a mid, central, tense vowel
3. Positions in words: initial, medial and final
4. Typical spellings: h**er**, d**ir**t, w**or**k, h**ur**t
5. Visible information: medium mouth opening, lips puckered or drawn up at the corners

[ɚ] Word List

Initial	*Medial*	*Final*
urge [ɚdʒ]	first [fɚst]	were [wɚ]
earn [ɚn]	serve [sɚv]	stir [stɚ]
err [ɚ]	curl [kɚl]	her [hɚ]
earnest ['ɚ nɪst]	clerk [klɚk]	over ['o vɚ]
early ['ɚ li]	heard [hɚd]	letter ['lɛt ɚ]

Contrasting Vowels and Diphthongs:

[ɚ]	[ə]		[ɚ]	[ɪɚ]
girl [gɚl]	— gull [gəl]		purr [pɚ]	— pier [pɪɚ]
third [θɚd]	— thud [θəd]		fur [fɚ]	— fear [fɪɚ]
stern [stɚn]	— stun [stən]		word [wɚd]	— weird [wɪɚd]
burn [bɚn]	— bun [bən]		burr [bɚ]	— beer [bɪɚ]
hurt [hɚt]	— hut [hət]		bird [bɚd]	— beard [bɪɚd]

[ə]

1. Phonetic symbol and I.D. number: [ə], V-7
2. Production information: a mid, central, lax vowel
3. Positions in words: initial, medial, and final
4. Typical spellings: **a**way, **o**ther, **u**s
5. Visible information: medium mouth opening, lips relaxed

[ə] Word List

Initial	*Medial*	*Final*
under ['ən dɚ]	mother ['məð ɚ]	data ['de tə]
other ['əð ɚ]	one [wən]	soda ['so də]
about [ə 'bæʊt]	balloon [bə 'lun]	vista ['vɪs tə]
oven [əvn]	love [ləv]	zebra ['zi brə]
asleep [ə 'slip]	done [dən]	arena [ə 'ri nə]

Contrasting Vowels:

[ə]		[ɪ]		[ə]		[ɑ]
love [ləv]	—	live [lɪv]		hut [hət]	—	hot [hɑt]
sunk [səŋk]	—	sink [sɪŋk]		luck [lək]	—	lock [lɑk]
rust [rəst]	—	wrist [rɪst]		shut [ʃət]	—	shot [ʃɑt]
bug [bəg]	—	big [bɪg]		putt [pət]	—	pot [pɑt]
truck [trək]	—	trick [trɪk]		bum [bəm]	—	bomb [bɑm]

---

[u]

1. Phonetic symbol and I.D. number: [u], V-8
2. Production information: a high, back, puckered, tense vowel
3. Positions in words: initial, medial, and final
4. Typical spellings: ch**ew**, d**o**, n**oo**n, tr**u**e
5. Visible information: narrow mouth opening, lips puckered

[u] Word List

Initial	*Medial*	*Final*
ooze [uz]	moon [mun]	shoe [ʃu]
oozed [uzd]	soon [sun]	too [tu]
oozing ['uz ɪŋ]	whose [huz]	who [hu]
	tomb [tum]	blue [blu]
	rule [rul]	grew [gru]

Contrasting Vowels and [u] and [ju]:

[u]		[ʊ]		[u]		[ju]
fool [ful]	—	full [fʊl]		food [fud]	—	feud [fjud]
cooed [kud]	—	could [kʊd]		coo [ku]	—	cue [kju]
wooed [wud]	—	would [wʊd]		moot [mut]	—	mute [mjut]
who'd [hud]	—	hood [hʊd]		booty ['bu ti]	—	beauty ['bju ti]
stewed [stud]	—	stood [stʊd]		whose [huz]	—	hues [hjuz]

[ʊ]

1. Phonetic symbol and I.D. number: [ʊ], V-9
2. Production information: a low-high, back, puckered, lax vowel
3. Position in words: medial
4. Typical spellings: l**oo**k, f**u**ll
5. Visible information: medium mouth opening, lips puckered

[ʊ] Word List

Medial
put [pʊt]
could [kʊd]
good [gʊd]
push [pʊʃ]
took [tʊk]

Contrasting Vowels:

[ʊ]		[ə]		[ʊ]		[o]
put [pʊt]	—	putt [pət]		full [fʊl]	—	foal [fol]
took [tʊk]	—	tuck [tək]		cook [kʊk]	—	coke [kok]
look [lʊk]	—	luck [lək]		pull [pʊl]	—	pole [pol]
book [bʊk]	—	buck [bək]		should [ʃʊd]	—	showed [ʃod]
could [kʊd]	—	cud [kəd]		brook [brʊk]	—	broke [brok]

---

[o]

1. Phonetic symbol and I.D. number: [o], V-10
2. Production information: a mid-back, puckered, tense vowel
3. Positions in words: initial, medial, and final
4. Typical spellings: g**o**, c**oa**t, c**o**de, t**oe**, sh**ow**
5. Visible information: contracting puckered movement

[o] Word List

Initial	*Medial*	*Final*
own [on]	soap [sop]	toe [to]
old [old]	both [boθ]	go [go]
oath [oθ]	known [non]	low [lo]
odor ['o dɚ]	wrote [rot]	foe [fo]
open ['o pn]	goes [goz]	though [ðo]

Contrasting Vowels:

[o]		[a]		[o]		[ɔ]
soak [sok]	—	sock [sak]		woke [wok]	—	walk [wɔk]
cope [kop]	—	cop [kap]		coal [kol]	—	call [kɔl]
robe [rob]	—	rob [rab]		loan [lon]	—	lawn [lɔn]
comb [kom]	—	calm [kam]		hole [hol]	—	haul [hɔl]
hope [hop]	—	hop [hap]		boat [bot]	—	bought [bɔt]

[ɔ]

1. Phonetic symbol and I.D. number: [ɔ], V-11
2. Production information: a low, back, puckered, tense vowel
3. Positions in words: initial, medial, and final
4. Typical spellings: **a**lso, **au**to, l**aw**
5. Visible information: wide mouth opening, lips puckered

[ɔ] Word List

Initial	*Medial*	*Final*
all [ɔl]	walk [wɔk]	law [lɔ]
auto ['ɔ to]	cause [kɔz]	jaw [dʒɔ]
office ['ɔ fɪs]	hawk [hɔk]	raw [rɔ]
author ['ɔ θɚ]	caught [kɔt]	thaw [θɔ]
awful ['ɔ fl]	fought [fɔt]	draw [drɔ]

Contrasting Vowels and Diphthongs:

[ɔ]	[ə]		[ɔ]	[ɔɪ]
gone [gɔn]	— gun [gən]		jaw [dʒɔ]	— joy [dʒɔɪ]
talk [tɔk]	— tuck [tək]		tall [tɔl]	— toil [tɔɪl]
caught [kɔt]	— cut [kət]		saw [sɔ]	— soy [sɔɪ]
pawn [pɔn]	— pun [pən]		all [ɔl]	— oil [ɔɪl]
balk [bɔk]	— buck [bək]		pause [pɔz]	— poise [pɔɪz]

[ɑ]

1. Phonetic symbol and I.D. number: [ɑ], V-12
2. Production information: low-low, back, lax vowel
3. Positions in words: initial and medial
4. Typical spelling: p**o**t, c**a**lm
5. Visible information: wide mouth opening, lips relaxed

[ɑ] Word List

Initial	*Medial*
honest ['ɑn ɪst]	doll [dɑl]
opera ['ɑp rə]	calm [kɑm]
art [ɑɚt]	upon [ə 'pɑn]
olive ['ɑl ɪv]	mop [mɑp]
arm [ɑɚm]	car [kɑɚ]

Contrasting Vowels:

[ɑ]	[æ]		[ɑ]	[ɔ]
mop [mɑp]	— map [mæp]		sod [sɑd]	— sawed [sɔd]
cot [kɑt]	— cat [kæt]		nod [nɑd]	— gnawed [nɔd]
pot [pɑt]	— pat [pæt]		hock [hɑk]	— hawk [hɔk]
hot [hɑt]	— hat [hæt]		car [kɑɚ]	— core [kɔɚ]
not [nɑt]	— gnat [næt]		pod [pɑd]	— pawed [pɔd]

[aɪ]

1. Phonetic symbol and I.D. number: [aɪ], D-12 and 2
2. Production information: the [a] sound followed by the [ɪ] sound
3. Positions in words: initial, medial, and final
4. Typical spellings: **i**vy, d**ie**, r**i**de, n**igh**t, b**y**
5. Visible information: wide-relaxed, followed by narrow relaxed

[aɪ] Word List

Initial	*Medial*	*Final*
idea [aɪ 'di ə]	kind [kaɪnd]	tie [taɪ]
eyes [aɪz]	cried [kraɪd]	buy [baɪ]
ivory ['aɪ vri]	light [laɪt]	guy [gaɪ]
aisle [aɪl]	guide [gaɪd]	my [maɪ]
idle [aɪdl]	fine [faɪn]	rye [raɪ]

Contrasting Vowels and Diphthongs:

[aɪ]	[a]		[aɪ]	[ɔɪ]
like [laɪk]	— lock [lak]		buy [baɪ]	— boy [bɔɪ]
wide [waɪd]	— wad [wad]		bile [baɪl]	— boil [bɔɪl]
type [taɪp]	— top [tap]		pint [paɪnt]	— point [pɔɪnt]
night [naɪt]	— knot [nat]		tile [taɪl]	— toil [tɔɪl]
tire [taɪɚ]	— tar [taɚ]		vice [vaɪs]	— voice [vɔɪs]

[æʊ]

1. Phonetic symbol and I.D. number: [æʊ], D-5 and 9
2. Production information: the [æ] sound followed by the [ʊ] sound
3. Positions in words: initial, medial, and final
4. Typical spellings: **ou**ch, h**ow**
5. Visible information: wide-spread, followed by a medium-puckered

[æʊ] Word List

Initial	*Medial*	*Final*
out [æʊt]	found [fæʊnd]	vow [væʊ]
hour [æʊɚ]	brown [bræʊn]	now [næʊ]
owl [æʊl]	house [hæʊs]	cow [kæʊ]
ouch [æʊtʃ]	loud [læʊd]	bough [bæʊ]
ounce [æʊns]	doubt [dæʊt]	allow [ə 'læʊ]

Contrasting Vowels and Diphthongs:

[æʊ]	[æ]		[æʊ]	[aɪ]
town [tæʊn]	— tan [tæn]		noun [næʊn]	— nine [naɪn]
pout [pæʊt]	— pat [pæt]		loud [læʊd]	— lied [laɪd]
rout [ræʊt]	— rat [ræt]		found [fæʊnd]	— find [faɪnd]
bout [bæʊt]	— bat [bæt]		mouse [mæʊs]	— mice [maɪs]
loud [læʊd]	— lad [læd]		tower [tæʊɚ]	— tire [taɪɚ]

[ɔɪ]

1. Phonetic symbol and I.D. number: [ɔɪ], D-11 and 2
2. Production information: the [ɔ] sound followed by the [ɪ] sound
3. Positions in words: initial, medial, and final
4. Typical spellings: b**oi**l, b**oy**
5. Visible information: wide-puckered, followed by a narrow-relaxed

[ɔɪ] Word List

Initial	Medial	Final
oil [ɔɪl]	point [pɔɪnt]	toy [tɔɪ]
ointment ['ɔɪnt mənt]	boil [bɔɪl]	joy [dʒɔɪ]
oyster ['ɔɪs tɚ]	noise [nɔɪz]	boy [bɔɪ]
oily ['ɔɪl i]	coin [kɔɪn]	annoy [ə 'nɔɪ]
oiler ['ɔɪl ɚ]	voice [vɔɪs]	employ [ɛm 'plɔɪ]

Contrasting Vowels and Diphthongs:

[ɔɪ]	[æʊ]		[ɔɪ]	[aɪ]
boy [bɔɪ]	—	bough [bæʊ]	boys [bɔɪz] — buys [baɪz]
coy [kɔɪ]	—	cow [kæʊ]	toyed [tɔɪd] — tied [taɪd]
foil [fɔɪl]	—	foul [fæʊl]	poise [pɔɪz] — pies [paɪz]
oil [ɔɪl]	—	owl [æʊl]	foil [fɔɪl] — file [faɪl]
ploy [plɔɪ]	—	plow [plæʊ]	boil [bɔɪl] — bile [baɪl]

THE CONSONANT SOUNDS OF AMERICAN ENGLISH

PRODUCTION

Table 4, page P-8, contains information for each of the twenty-five American English consonant sounds, explaining how each sound is produced. The phonetic symbol for each sound is enclosed in brackets and the spelling equivalent is also indicated if it differs from the phonetic symbol.

It should be noted that some of the consonant sounds are voiceless (Vs), which means they are produced without vocal fold vibration, and others are voiced (V), and are produced with vocal fold vibration. The consonant sounds are also differentiated by their place of articulation, which indicates where the shaping of the sounds takes place. Lastly, the consonant sounds are classified by their manner of formation, or how they are produced.

1. THE STOP-PLOSIVE SOUNDS:

The [p] [b], [t] [d], and [k] [g] sounds are described as stop-plosive sounds because of their manner of formation, which can result in an audible release of air that sounds like a small "explosion." When these sounds are produced at the beginning of a word or syllable, they function as releasing consonants and are produced as plosive sounds. When these sounds are produced at the end of a word or syllable, they function as arresting consonants and may be produced as a stop or a plosive.

When these sounds are produced as plosives, the exhaled breath stream is blocked by the lips or tongue and air pressure is built up in the oral cavity and released when the articulators are separated. The released air can be heard for both the voiceless and voiced plosive sounds, but is stronger for the voiceless sounds. The bilabial plosives are produced with the greatest release of air and the velar plosives with the least amount of air released.

If the palm of the hand or several fingers are placed in front of the lips, a release of air can be felt when the sounds are produced. The vocal fold vibration for the voiced sounds can be felt by putting the thumb and index finger on the larynx. Voicing can also be heard very distinctly when the ears are closed with the fingers.

When the plosive sounds are produced as stops, the articulators make contact, but no buildup of pressure or release of air takes place. When the sounds are produced as stops they are less easily identified by the listener than when produced as plosive sounds.

2. THE FRICATIVE SOUNDS:

The [ʍ], [f] [v], [θ] [ð], [s] [z], [ʃ] [ʒ], and [h] sounds are described as fricative sounds, because of the audible friction noises that result when the exhaled air, under pressure, passes between surfaces or through spaces of different size or shape.

The fricative sounds, like the stop-plosive sounds, often come in pairs with the same place of articulation, one being voiceless and the other voiced. The voiceless sound of the pair will have more air flow than the voiced one and will have a stronger friction sound. The fricative sounds produced with smaller openings will tend to be higher-pitched sounds.

3. THE AFFRICATE SOUNDS:

The affricate sounds [tʃ] [dʒ] are sounds produced as a fusion of a plosive sound followed by a fricative sound. The place of articulation of the tongue moves from the alveolar ridge for the plosive sound to the alveolar palatal position for the fricative sound. Like the stop-plosive and fricative sounds, the affricates are produced with a buildup of breath pressure and a release of air, which is greater for the voiceless sound. The affricate sounds are some times referred to as "affricative" sounds.

4. THE NASAL SOUNDS:

The nasal sounds [m] [n] [ŋ] are voiced sounds that are resonated in both the oral and nasal cavities. The nasal resonance can be felt by placing the thumb and index fingers on the bones of the nose where the vibration can be felt. The nasal quality can be observed by pinching and releasing the nostrils while the sound is being produced. This variation in sound will not be present in the absence of nasal resonance or in the normal production of the American English vowel, diphthong, and triphthong sounds or other voiced consonant sounds.

5. THE GLIDE SOUNDS:

The glides [w] [l] [r] [j] are voiced sounds that are sometimes referred to as "semivowels." When they are produced as releasing consonants at the beginning of words or syllables they are produced as movements of the articulators, moving or gliding to the following vowel, diphthong, or triphthong sound. When the [l] and [r] sounds are produced in the arresting position, at the end of words or syllables, they function as vowel sounds and the tongue moves to the place of articulation rather than away from it.

Additional specific information about each consonant sound of the language will be found with the word lists for each sound.

THE CONSONANT AND CONSONANT BLEND SOUNDS OF AMERICAN ENGLISH

PRONUNCIATION

The following exercises, which primarily focus on the consonant sounds of American English, utilize the pronunciation of a native speaker of American English as a model. You can use either the audiocassette recorded for use with this book or the services of an American English speaker who will read the lists of sounds and words in the tables that follow. The model speaker should pronounce the lists of words clearly and *naturally*. The speaker should *not* pronounce each syllable separately and should not emphasize any syllable that is not normally emphasized. Normal and natural American English is the goal.

Please turn to Table 4 on page P-8. Column 2 contains the IPA symbol in brackets for each of the consonant sounds of English. Please note in column 1 the identification number of each sound, which corresponds to the alphabetical sequence of the consonant sound symbols. Please listen to side 2 of the audiocassette or ask your model speaker to read from the columns as instructed below.

OBJECTIVE 1. To learn the phonetic symbol that represents each of the consonant sounds.

Procedures:

A. As the model speaker says each consonant sound in isolation or combined with a vowel sound, listen carefully and point to the phonetic symbol in column 2 that represents that sound. Play the tape or ask an American English speaker to pronounce the sounds in column 2 in order. (The English speaker can identify the correct sound by saying first the example words in columns 4, 5, and 6.)

B. As the model speaker says each sound, write down the correct phonetic symbol and I.D. number. Repeat this procedure until you feel comfortable with the symbols.

OBJECTIVE 2. To be able to identify the correct consonant symbols when the sounds are presented in random order or grouped by their manner of production.

Procedures:

A. As the model speaker says the sounds in column 2 in random order or in specific groups, listen carefully and point to the proper symbols. (Play the tape or ask an American English speaker to pronounce the sounds in random order or grouped by manner of production.)

B. The model speaker on the audiotape will identify the correct symbol by saying the I.D. number. (The English speaker can simply point to the correct symbol.)

OBJECTIVE 3. To be able to listen to two consonant sounds and decide correctly if the same sound was heard twice or if different sounds were heard.

Procedures:

A. Listen to paired consonant sounds. B. Decide I.D. numbers of sounds heard. C. Listen to correct I.D. numbers. D. Repeat as necessary. (Use the audiotape or a model speaker.)

OBJECTIVE 4. To learn to correctly imitate each consonant sound.

Procedures:

A. Listen to the sound. B. Imitate sound out loud. C. Point to its phonetic symbol. D. Write symbol. E. Listen for correct I.D. number. F. Repeat as necessary. (Use the audiotape or a model speaker.)

OBJECTIVE 5. To listen to the correct production of word lists for each consonant sound of American English in the various word positions in which they occur. To learn how to read the phonetic transcriptions of the words and to say them with correct pronunciation.

Procedures:

A. Turn to page P-30 for the word lists for consonant [p]. B. Listen to the words for the [p] sound in the initial position. C. Imitate each word while looking at its phonetic transcription. D. Continue with word lists for other positions and those with contrasting sounds. E. Continue with the word lists for the other consonants with the same manner of production and then other manners of production. F. Repeat as often as necessary. (Use the audiotape or a model speaker.)

[p]

1. Phonetic symbol and I.D. number: [p], C-13
2. Production information: a voiceless, bilabial stop-plosive sound the cognate of [b]
3. Positions in words: initial, medial, and final
4. Typical spellings: **p**eak, su**pp**er, ri**pe**
5. Use as a silent letter of the alphabet: **p**salm, **p**sychic, **p**sychosis
6. Visible information: lips opening from closed position (same as [b] and [m])
7. Initial blends: [pl] play; [pr] price; [sp] speak; [spl] splash
8. Final blends: [ps] wipes, cups; [pt] stopped, wiped

[p] Word List

Initial	Medial	Final
pet [pɛt]	apple [æpl]	rope [rop]
pole ['pol]	rapid ['ræp ɪd]	cap [kæp]
pack [pæk]	carpet ['kɑɚ pɪt]	help [hɛlp]
pull [pʊl]	report [rɪ 'pɔɚt]	jump [dʒəmp]
palm [pɑm]	oppose [ə 'poz]	stop [stɑp]

Contrasting Consonants:

[p]		[f]		[p]		[b]
pour [pɔɚ]	—	four [fɔɚ]		pair [pɛɚ]	—	bear [bɛɚ]
peel [pil]	—	feel [fil]		pat [pæt]	—	bat [bæt]
pin [pɪn]	—	fin [fɪn]		pill [pɪl]	—	bill [bɪl]
pit [pɪt]	—	fit [fɪt]		plank [plæŋk]	—	blank [blæŋk]
plea [pli]	—	flea [fli]		pride [praɪd]	—	bride [braɪd]

[b]

1. Phonetic symbol and I.D. number: [b], C-1
2. Production information: a voiced, bilabial stop-plosive sound, the cognate of [p]
3. Positions in words: initial, medial, and final
4. Typical spellings: **be**, ri**bb**on, ro**b**e
5. Use as a silent letter of the alphabet: bom**b**, num**b**, lim**b**, com**b**, de**b**t
6. Visible information: lips opening from closed position (same as [p] and [m])
7. Initial blends: [bl] blue, black; [br] brown, bring; [bj] beauty
8. Final blends: [bz] cabs, ribs; [bd] robbed, robed

[b] Word List

Initial	*Medial*	*Final*
ball [bɔl]	rabbit ['ræb ɪt]	web [wɛb]
been [bɪn]	robber ['rɑb ɚ]	cab [kæb]
box [bɑks]	above [ə 'bəv]	rib [rɪb]
barn [bɑɚn]	number ['nəm bɚ]	robe [rob]
be [bi]	about [ə 'bæʊt]	rob [rɑb]

Contrasting Consonants:

[b]	[p]		[b]	[d]
bath [bæθ]	— path [pæθ]		bait [bet]	— date [det]
beer [bɪɚ]	— peer [pɪɚ]		bent [bɛnt]	— dent [dɛnt]
bees [biz]	— peas [piz]		bore [bɔɚ]	— door [dɔɚ]
cab [kæb]	— cap [kæp]		bribe [braɪb]	— bride [braɪd]
lab [læb]	— lap [læp]		robe [rob]	— rode [rod]

[t]

1. Phonetic symbol and I.D. number: [t], C-17
2. Production information: a voiceless, alveolar stop-plosive, the cognate of [d]
3. Positions in words: initial, medial, and final
4. Typical spellings: to, better, note
5. Use as a silent letter of the alphabet: listen, fasten
6. Visible information: the front of the tongue touching the upper gum ridge (same as [d] and [n])
7. Initial blends: [tr] try, treat; [tw] twin, twelve; [st] stop
8. Final blends: [ts] pets, puts; [ft] left; [kt] liked; [st] cost

[t] Word List

Initial	Medial	Final
tie [taɪ]	party ['paɚ ti]	cut [kət]
tree [tri]	after ['æf tɚ]	fast [fæst]
tool [tul]	latter ['læt ɚ]	left [lɛft]
tip [tɪp]	pretty ['prɪt i]	cat [kæt]
town [tæʊn]	sister ['sɪs tɚ]	liked [laɪkt]

Contrasting Consonants:

[t]		[d]	[t]		[θ]
tear [tɪɚ]	—	dear [dɪɚ]	tin [tɪn]	—	thin [θɪn]
time [taɪm]	—	dime [daɪm]	true [tru]	—	threw [θru]
writing ['raɪt ɪŋ]	—	riding ['raɪd ɪŋ]	eater ['it ɚ]	—	ether ['i θɚ]
waiting ['wet ɪŋ]	—	wading ['wed ɪŋ]	debt [dɛt]	—	death [dɛθ]
mat [mæt]	—	mad [mæd]	boat [bot]	—	both [boθ]

[d]

1. Phonetic symbol and I.D. number: [d], C-3
2. Production information: a voiced, alveolar stop-plosive sound, the cognate of [t].
3. Positions in words: initial, medial, and final
4. Typical spellings: **d**eep, la**dd**er, ri**de**
5. Visible information: the front of the tongue touching the upper gum ridge (same as [t] and [n])
7. Initial blends: [dr] drink, dry; [dw] dwarf, dwindle
8. Final blends: [dz] beds, feeds; [bd] bribed, sobbed

[d] Word List

Initial	Medial	Final
down [dæʊn]	window ['wɪn do]	food [fud]
dress [drɛs]	louder ['læʊd ɚ]	hand [hænd]
dear [dɪɚ]	radio ['re di ˌo]	bread [brɛd]
door [dɔɚ]	candy ['kæn di]	hide [haɪd]
do [du]	today [tə 'de]	find [faɪnd]

Contrasting Consonants:

[d]	[t]		[d]	[dʒ]
do [du]	— to [tu]		dam [dæm]	— jam [dʒæm]
done [dən]	— ton [tən]		aiding ['ed ɪŋ]	— aging ['edʒ ɪŋ]
down [dæʊn]	— town [tæʊn]		paid [ped]	— page [pedʒ]
padding ['pæd ɪŋ]	— patting ['pæt ɪŋ]		debt [dɛt]	— jet [dʒɛt]
need [nid]	— neat [nit]		bud [bəd]	— budge [bədʒ]

[k]

1. Phonetic symbol and I.D. number: [k], C-8
2. Production information: a voiceless, velar stop-plosive sound the cognate of [g]
3. Positions in words: initial, medial, and final
4. Typical spellings: **k**ill, ma**k**e, **c**ap, ac**c**ount, ne**ck**
5. Use as a silent letter of the alphabet: **k**now, **k**not, **k**nack
6. Visible information: lifting of the adam's apple, frequently identified by context (same as [g])
7. Initial blends: [kl] clean, class; [kr] cross, cry
8. Final blends: [ks] books, makes; [kt] looked, talked

[k] Word List

Initial	Medial	Final
come [kəm]	walking ['wɔk ɪŋ]	cook [kʊk]
cool [kul]	picnic ['pɪk nɪk]	take [tek]
count [kæʊnt]	likely ['lɑɪk li]	look [lʊk]
can [kæn]	second ['sɛk nd]	milk [mɪlk]
catch [kætʃ]	biscuit ['bɪs kɪt]	work [wɚk]

Contrasting Consonants:

[k]	[g]		[k]	[t]
cab [kæb] —	gab [gæb]		key [ki] —	tea [ti]
core [kɔɚ] —	gore [gɔɚ]		kick [kɪk] —	tick [tɪk]
backing ['bæk ɪŋ] —	bagging ['bæg ɪŋ]		kill [kɪl] —	till [tɪl]
tacking ['tæk ɪŋ] —	tagging ['tæg ɪŋ]		can [kæn] —	tan [tæn]
tack [tæk] —	tag [tæg]		back [bæk] —	bat [bæt]

[g]

1. Phonetic symbol and I.D. number: [g], C-5
2. Production information: a voiced, velar stop-plosive sound, the cognate of [k].
3. Positions in words: initial, medial, and final
4. Typical spellings: **go**, e**gg**
5. Use as a silent letter of the alphabet: si**g**n, rin**g**
6. Visible information: lifting of the adam's apple, frequently identified by context (same as [k])
7. Initial blends: [gl] glad, glue; [gr] group, grey
8. Final blends: [gd] begged, fogged; [gz] bugs, digs

[g] Word List

Initial	*Medial*	*Final*
guess [gɛs]	legal ['li gl]	leg [lɛg]
gone [gɔn]	ago [ə 'go]	bug [bəg]
got [gɑt]	began [bɪ 'gæn]	egg [ɛg]
gun [gən]	forget [fɚ 'gɛt]	dig [dɪg]
game [gem]	organ [ɔɚ 'gn]	fog [fɑg]

Contrasting Consonants:

[g]	[k]		[gl]	[kr]
goal [gol]	— coal [kol]		glue [glu]	— crew [kru]
gap [gæp]	— cap [kæp]		glow [glo]	— crow [kro]
goat [got]	— coat [kot]		[gl]	[kl]
rag [ræg]	— rack [ræk]		glass [glæs]	— class [klæs]
nag [næg]	— knack [næk]		[gr]	[kr]
			great [gret]	— crate [kret]
			grab [græb]	— crab [kræb]

[ʍ]

1. Phonetic symbol and I.D. number: [ʍ], C-22
2. Production information: a voiceless, bilabial fricative sound
3. Positions in words: initial and medial
4. Typical spelling: **wh**ile
5. Visible information: the lips being drawn together or puckered (same as [w])

[ʍ] Word List

Initial	*Medial*
when [ʍɛn]	awhile [ə 'ʍaɪl]
where [ʍɛɚ]	nowhere ['no ˌʍɛɚ]
what [ʍət]	everywhere ['ɛv ri ˌʍɛɚ]
why [ʍaɪ]	somewhat ['səm ˌʍət]
which [ʍɪtʃ]	somewhere ['səm ˌʍɛɚ]

Contrasting Consonants:

[ʍ]	[w]		[ʍ]	[h]
where [ʍɛɚ] —	wear [wɛɚ]		whim [ʍɪm] —	him [hɪm]
whine [ʍaɪn] —	wine [waɪn]		which [ʍɪtʃ] —	hitch [hɪtʃ]
which [ʍɪtʃ] —	witch [wɪtʃ]		when [ʍɛn] —	hen [hɛn]
wheel [ʍil] —	we'll [wil]		whack [ʍæk] —	hack [hæk]
whether ['ʍɛð ɚ] —	weather ['wɛð ɚ]		white [ʍaɪt] —	height [haɪt]

[f]

1. Phonetic symbol and I.D. number: [f], C-4
2. Production information: a voiceless, labio-dental fricative, the cognate of [v]
3. Positions in words: initial, medial, and final
4. Typical spellings: **f**eet, cu**ff**, sa**f**e, tou**gh**, **ph**one
5. Visible information: movement of the lower lip to the upper teeth (same as [v])
6. Initial blends: [fl] flight, flat; [fr] fruit, free
7. Final blends: [fs] coughs, loafs; [ft] staffed, left

[f] Word List

Initial	Medial	Final
for [fɔɚ]	coffee ['kɔ fi]	life [laɪf]
fat [fæt]	suffer ['səf ɚ]	off [ɔf]
first [fɚst]	effort ['ɛf ɚt]	safe [sef]
fool [ful]	afraid [ə 'fred]	knife [naɪf]
find [faɪnd]	careful ['kɛɚ fl]	cough [kɔf]

Contrasting Consonants:

[f]	[v]	[f]	[θ]
fat [fæt] —	vat [væt]	free [fri] —	three [θri]
fine [faɪn] —	vine [vaɪn]	frill [frɪl] —	thrill [θrɪl]
fast [fæst] —	vast [væst]	roofless ['ruf lɪs] —	ruthless ['ruθ lɪs]
half [hæf] —	have [hæv]	deaf [dɛf] —	death [dɛθ]
safe [sef] —	save [sev]	reef [rif] —	wreath [riθ]

[v]

1. Phonetic symbol and I.D. number: [v], C-20
2. Production information: a voiced, labio-dental fricative, the cognate of [f]
3. Positions in words: initial, medial, and final
4. Typical spellings: vase, dive
5. Visible information: movement of the lower lip to the upper teeth (same as [f])
6. Final blends: [vd] loved, dived; [vz] lives, gives

[v] Word List

Initial	Medial	Final
visit ['vɪz ɪt]	never ['nɛv ɚ]	five [fɑɪv]
very ['vɛɚ i]	ever ['ɛv ɚ]	drive [drɑɪv]
view [vju]	diving ['dɑɪv ɪŋ]	stove [stov]
vowel [væʊl]	seven [sɛvn]	have [hæv]
veil [vel]	cover ['kəv ɚ]	move [muv]

Contrasting Consonants:

[v]		[f]		[v]		[b]
vase [ves]	—	face [fes]		very ['vɛɚ i]	—	berry ['bɛɚ i]
vast [væst]	—	fast [fæst]		vent [vɛnt]	—	bent [bɛnt]
vat [væt]	—	fat [fæt]		vote [vot]	—	boat [bot]
have [hæv]	—	half [hæf]		veil [vel]	—	bail [bel]
save [sev]	—	safe [sef]		vest [vɛst]	—	best [bɛst]

[θ]

1. Phonetic symbol and I.D. number: [θ], C-18
2. Production information: a voiceless, inter-dental fricative sound, the cognate of [ð]
3. Positions in words: initial, medial, and final
4. Typical spelling: **th**ing
5. Visible information: the tip of the tongue showing between the front teeth (same as [ð])
6. Initial blends: [θr] three, throat
7. Final blends: [θs] deaths, months

[θ] Word List

Initial	Medial	Final
think [θɪŋk]	birthday ['bɚθ ˌde]	north [nɔɚθ]
three [θri]	healthy ['hɛl θi]	south [sæʊθ]
thank [θæŋk]	anything ['ɛn i ˌθɪŋ]	bath [bæθ]
thin [θɪn]	something ['səm θɪŋ]	teeth [tiθ]
thick [θɪk]	everything ['ɛv ri ˌθɪŋ]	month [mənθ]

Contrasting Consonants:

[θ]	[s]		[θ]	[t]
thick [θɪk] —	sick [sɪk]		thank [θæŋk] —	tank [tæŋk]
thing [θɪŋ] —	sing [sɪŋ]		thigh [θaɪ] —	tie [taɪ]
thin [θɪn] —	sin [sɪn]		thinker ['θɪŋk ɚ] —	tinker ['tɪŋk ɚ]
think [θɪŋk] —	sink [sɪŋk]		thought [θɔt] —	taught [tɔt]
thank [θæŋk] —	sank [sæŋk]		three [θri] —	tree [tri]

[ð]

1. Phonetic symbol and I.D. number: [ð], C-19
2. Production information: a voiced inter-dental fricative sound
   the cognate of [θ]
3. Positions in words: initial, medial, and final
4. Typical spellings: **th**em, tee**the**
5. Visible information: the tip of the tongue showing between the fron
   teeth (same as [θ])
6. Final blends: [ðd] breathed, bathed; [ðz] breathes, bathes

[ð] Word List

Initial	*Medial*	*Final*
this [ðɪs]	mother ['məð ɚ]	breathe [brið]
that [ðæt]	brother ['brəð ɚ]	smooth [smuð]
the [ðə]	another [ə 'nəð ɚ]	clothe [kloð]
them [ðɛm]	weather ['wɛð ɚ]	teethe [tið]
those [ðoz]	bother ['bɑð ɚ]	wreathe [rið]

Contrasting Consonants:

[ð]		[θ]		[ð]		[d]
teethe [tið]	—	teeth [tiθ]		then [ðɛn]	—	den [dɛn]
bathe [beð]	—	bath [bæθ]		they [ðe]	—	day [de]
wreathe [rið]	—	wreath [riθ]		there [ðɛɚ]	—	dare [dɛɚ]
either ['i ðɚ]	—	ether ['i θɚ]		though [ðo]	—	dough [do]
sheathe [ʃið]	—	sheath [ʃiθ]		those [ðoz]	—	dose [doz]

[s]

1. Phonetic symbol and I.D. number: [s], C-15
2. Production information: a voiceless, alveolar fricative sound, the cognate of [z]
3. Positions in words: initial, medial, and final
4. Typical spellings: sit, loss, loose, city, nice
5. Visible information: narrow mouth opening, teeth close together, lips spread (same as [z])
6. Initial blends: [sk] skin; [sl] slip; [sm] smoke; [sn] snow; [sp] speak
7. Final blends: [sk] task; [sp] lisp; [st] last; [sps] grasps; [sks] risks

[s] Word List

Initial	Medial	Final
school [skul]	lesson [lɛsn]	miss [mɪs]
sing [sɪŋ]	listen [lɪsn]	us [əs]
said [sɛd]	mister ['mɪs tɚ]	nice [nɑɪs]
six [sɪks]	missing ['mɪs ɪŋ]	once [wəns]
sat [sæt]	eraser [ə 'res ɚ]	pass [pæs]

Contrasting Consonants:

[s]		[z]		[s]		[ʃ]
seal [sil]	—	zeal [zil]		sock [sɑk]	—	shock [ʃɑk]
sip [sɪp]	—	zip [zɪp]		seat [sit]	—	sheet [ʃit]
sag [sæg]	—	zag [zæg]		gas [gæs]	—	gash [gæʃ]
bus [bəs]	—	buzz [bəz]		mass [mæs]	—	mash [mæʃ]
loose [lus]	—	lose [luz]		class [klæs]	—	clash [klæʃ]

[z]

1. Phonetic symbol and I.D. number: [z], C-24
2. Production information: a voiced, alveolar fricative sound, the cognate of [s]
3. Positions in words: initial, medial, and final
4. Typical spellings: zipper, buzz, prize, easy, rise
5. Visible information: narrow mouth opening, teeth close together, lips spread (same as [s])
6. Final blends: [zd] pleased, used; [bz] cabs; [dz] seeds; [gz] bugs; [lz] calls; [mz] names; [nz] coins; [vz] lives

[z] Word List

Initial	Medial	Final
zero ['zɪɚ o]	dozen ['də zn]	has [hæz]
zoo [zu]	easy ['i zi]	nose [noz]
zone [zon]	lazy ['le zi]	size [saɪz]
zeal [zil]	music ['mju zɪk]	as [æz]
zest [zɛst]	dizzy ['dɪz i]	use [juz]

Contrasting Consonants:

[z]	[s]		[z]	[ð]
raising ['rez ɪŋ] —	racing ['res ɪŋ]	bays [bez] —	bathe [beð]
razor ['rez ɚ] —	racer ['res ɚ]	tease [tiz] —	teethe [tið]
prizes ['praɪz ɪz] —	prices ['praɪs ɪz]	lays [lez] —	lathe [leð]
muzzle [məzl] —	muscle [məsl]		[z]	[ðz]
lazy ['le zi] —	lacy ['les i]	close [kloz] —	clothes [kloðz]
		ties [taɪz] —	tithes [taɪðz]

[ʃ]

1. Phonetic symbol and I.D. number: [ʃ], C-16
2. Production information: a voiceless, alveolar-palatal fricative sound, the cognate of [ʒ]
3. Positions in words: initial, medial, and final
4. Typical spellings: **s**ure, pre**ss**ure, **sh**oe, mo**ti**on, ra**ci**al, o**c**ean
5. Visible information: lips are thrust forward or projected (same as [ʒ], [tʃ], and [dʒ])
6. Initial blends: [ʃr] **shr**ine, **shr**imp
7. Final blends: [ʃt] pu**shed**, ca**shed**

[ʃ] Word List

Initial	*Medial*	*Final*
shop [ʃɑp]	machine [mə ˈʃin]	wash [wɑʃ]
should [ʃʊd]	ocean [ˈo ʃn]	push [pʊʃ]
shut [ʃət]	motion [ˈmo ʃn]	fish [fɪʃ]
shine [ʃɑɪn]	fishing [ˈfɪʃ ɪŋ]	dish [dɪʃ]
shout [ʃæʊt]	ashamed [ə ˈʃemd]	cash [kæʃ]

Contrasting Consonants:

[ʃ]		[tʃ]		[ʃ]		[s]
ship [ʃɪp]	—	chip [tʃɪp]		shave [ʃev]	—	save [sev]
shoe [ʃu]	—	chew [tʃu]		shake [ʃek]	—	sake [sek]
shin [ʃɪn]	—	chin [tʃɪn]		shed [ʃɛd]	—	said [sɛd]
cash [kæʃ]	—	catch [kætʃ]		mesh [mɛʃ]	—	mess [mɛs]
wish [wɪʃ]	—	witch [wɪtʃ]		fashion [fæʃn]	—	fasten [fæsn]

[ʒ]

1. Phonetic symbol and I.D. number: [ʒ], C-25
2. Production information: a voiced, alveolar-palatal fricative sound, the cognate of [ʃ]
3. Positions in words: initial, medial, and final
4. Typical spellings: vision, measure, garage, seizure
5. Visible information: lips are thrust forward or projected (same as [ʃ], [tʃ] [dʒ])
6. Final blends: [ʒd] garaged, camouflaged

[ʒ] Word List

Initial	Medial	Final
genre ['ʒan rə]	usual ['ju ʒu əl]	mirage [mɪ 'rɑʒ]
	casual ['kæʒ u əl]	corsage [kɔɚ 'sɑʒ]
	vision [vɪʒn]	beige [beʒ]
	visual ['vɪʒ u əl]	rouge [ruʒ]
	seizure ['si ʒɚ]	prestige [prɛs 'tiʒ]

Contrasting Consonants:

[ʒ]		[dʒ]
lesion ['li ʒn]	—	legion ['li dʒn]
version ['vɚ ʒn]	—	virgin ['vɚ dʒn]

---

[h]

1. Phonetic symbol and I.D. number: [h], C-6
2. Production information: a voiceless, glottal fricative sound.
3. Positions in words: initial and medial
4. Typical spelling: hand
5. Use as a silent letter of the alphabet: honor, hours, ghost
6. Visible information: no visible component, must be obtained from context

[h] Word List

Initial	Medial
he [hi]	behave [bɪ 'hev]
hello [hɛ 'lo]	anyhow ['ɛn i ˌhæʊ]
half [hæf]	ahead [ə 'hɛd]
hear [hɪɚ]	behind [bɪ 'hɑɪnd]
horse [hɔɚs]	perhaps [pɚ 'hæps]

Contrasting Consonants:

[h]		[ʍ]		[h]		[æ, i, ɪ]
hair [hɛɚ]	—	where [ʍɛɚ]		hat [hæt]	—	at [æt]
hip [hɪp]	—	whip [ʍɪp]		heat [hit]	—	eat [it]
heat [hit]	—	wheat [ʍit]		had [hæd]	—	add [æd]
hail [hel]	—	whale [ʍel]		has [hæz]	—	as [æz]
heel [hil]	—	wheel [ʍil]		hear [hɪɚ]	—	ear [ɪɚ]

[tʃ]

1. Phonetic symbol and I.D. number: [tʃ], C-2
2. Production information: a voiceless, alveolar-palatal affricate sound, the cognate of [dʒ]
3. Positions in words: initial, medial, and final
4. Typical spellings: **ch**ain, ca**tch**, na**t**ure, men**t**ion
5. Visible information: lips are thrust forward or projected (same as [dʒ], [ʃ] and [ʒ])
6. Final blends: [tʃt] perched, reached; [ntʃt] lunched, pinched

[tʃ] Word List

Initial	Medial	Final
chew [tʃu]	kitchen [kɪtʃn]	lunch [ləntʃ]
chair [tʃɛɚ]	pitcher ['pɪtʃɚ]	catch [kætʃ]
chase [tʃes]	teaching ['titʃɪŋ]	much [mətʃ]
check [tʃɛk]	butcher ['bʊtʃɚ]	reach [ritʃ]
change [tʃendʒ]	ketchup ['kɛtʃəp]	rich [rɪtʃ]

Contrasting Consonants:

[tʃ]	[ʃ]		[tʃ]	[dʒ]
cheap [tʃip] —	sheep [ʃip]	chunk [tʃəŋk] —	junk [dʒəŋk]
cheat [tʃit] —	sheet [ʃit]	chin [tʃɪn] —	gin [dʒɪn]
watching ['watʃɪŋ] —	washing ['waʃɪŋ]		
catch [kætʃ] —	cash [kæʃ]	rich [rɪtʃ] —	ridge [rɪdʒ]
ditch [dɪtʃ] —	dish [dɪʃ]	choke [tʃok] —	joke [dʒok]
		batch [bætʃ] —	badge [bædʒ]

[dʒ]

1. Phonetic symbol and I.D. number: [dʒ], C-7
2. Production information: a voiced, alveolar-palatal affricate sound, the cognate of [tʃ]
3. Positions in words: initial, medial, and final
4. Typical spellings: **j**oin, ma**g**ic, ca**ge**, lo**dg**ing, ba**dge**, a**g**ent, sol**d**ier
5. Visible information: lips are thrust forward or projected
6. Final blends: [dʒd] caged, paged; [ndʒd] hinged, ranged

[dʒ] Word List

Initial	*Medial*	*Final*
jar [dʒɑɚ]	magic ['mædʒ ɪk]	edge [ɛdʒ]
jacket ['dʒæk ɪt]	soldier ['sol dʒɚ]	large [lɑɚdʒ]
juice [dʒus]	engine ['ɛn dʒn]	bridge [brɪdʒ]
just [dʒəst]	agent ['e dʒənt]	huge [hjudʒ]
jail [dʒel]	region ['ri dʒn]	cage [kedʒ]

Contrasting Consonants:

[dʒ]		[tʃ]	[dʒ]		[z]
jest [dʒɛst]	—	chest [tʃɛst]	gypped [dʒɪpt]	—	zipped [zɪpt]
gyp [dʒɪp]	—	chip [tʃɪp]	jealous ['dʒɛl əs]	—	zealous ['zɛl əs]
jeer [dʒɪɚ]	—	cheer [tʃɪɚ]	budged [bədʒd]	—	buzzed [bəzd]
edge [ɛdʒ]	—	etch [ɛtʃ]	raging ['redʒ ɪŋ]	—	raising ['rez ɪŋ]
lunge [ləndʒ]	—	lunch [ləntʃ]	wage [wedʒ]	—	ways [wez]

[m]

1. Phonetic symbol and I.D. number: [m], C-10
2. Production information: a voiced, bilabial nasal sound.
3. Positions in words: initial, medial, and final
4. Typical spellings: **m**e, su**mm**er, na**m**e
5. Visible information: lips opening from a closed position (same as [p] and [b])
6. Initial blends: [sm] smile, small
7. Final blends: [md] named, combed; [mz] comes, dimes; [mp] lamp, stamp; [mpt] camped, limped; [mps] jumps, camps

[m] Word List

Initial	Medial	Final
mast [mæst]	farmer [ˈfɑɚm ɚ]	some [səm]
might [mɑɪt]	almost [ˈɔl most]	time [tɑɪm]
may [me]	hammer [ˈhæm ɚ]	came [kem]
mood [mud]	coming [ˈkəm ɪŋ]	from [frəm]
make [mek]	empty [ˈɛmp ti]	climb [klɑɪm]

Contrasting Consonants:

[m]		[b]	[m]		[b]
make [mek]	—	bake [bek]	rum [rəm]	—	rub [rəb]
mill [mɪl]	—	bill [bɪl]	Mom [mɑm]	—	mob [mɑb]
match [mætʃ]	—	batch [bætʃ]	roam [rom]	—	robe [rob]
meat [mit]	—	beat [bit]	rim [rɪm]	—	rib [rɪb]
mug [məg]	—	bug [bəg]	psalm [sɑm]	—	sob [sɑb]

[n]

1. Phonetic symbol and I.D. number: [n], C-11
2. Production information: a voiced, alveolar nasal sound
3. Positions in words: initial, medial, and final
4. Typical spellings: **n**ot, fu**nn**y, o**n**e
5. Visible information: the front of the tongue touching the upper gum ridge (same as [t] and [d])
7. Initial blend: [sn] snow, sniff
8. Final blends: [nd] bend, burned; [nz] cans, trains; [ns] once, fence [nt] went, paint; [nts] pants, wants; [ntʃ] pinch, ranch; [ndʒ] range lounge

[n] Word List

Initial	Medial	Final
new [nu]	many ['mɛn i]	sun [sən]
knee [ni]	under ['ən dɚ]	fun [fən]
night [naɪt]	any ['ɛn i]	on [ɔn]
nest [nɛst]	raining ['ren ɪŋ]	ten [tɛn]
near [nɪɚ]	into ['ɪn tu]	ran [ræn]

Contrasting Consonants:

[n]		[d]	[n]		[ŋ]
noun [næʊn]	—	down [dæʊn]	win [wɪn]	—	wing [wɪŋ]
need [nid]	—	deed [did]	sin [sɪn]	—	sing [sɪŋ]
nip [nɪp]	—	dip [dɪp]	thin [θɪn]	—	thing [θɪŋ]
nor [nɔɚ]	—	door [dɔɚ]	ran [ræn]	—	rang [ræŋ]
rain [ren]	—	raid [red]	lawn [lɔn]	—	long [lɔŋ]

[ŋ]

1. Phonetic symbol and I.D. number: [ŋ], C-12
2. Production information: a voiced, velar nasal sound
3. Positions in words: medial and final
4. Typical spellings: si**ng**, ba**n**k
5. Visible information: identified by context
6. Final blends: [ŋd] hanged, ringed; [ŋz] sings, things; [ŋk] think, sink; [ŋks] thanks, banks; [ŋkt] banked, honked

[ŋ] Word List

Medial	*Final*
singer ['sɪŋ ɚ]	sang [sæŋ]
banker ['bæŋk ɚ]	going ['go ɪŋ]
monkey ['mən ki]	lung [ləŋ]
ringing ['rɪŋ ɪŋ]	making ['mek ɪŋ]
single ['sɪŋ gl]	long [lɔŋ]

Contrasting Consonants:

[ŋ]	[g]		[ŋ]	[ŋk]
rang [ræŋ]	— rag [ræg]		sing [sɪŋ]	— sink [sɪŋk]
hung [həŋ]	— hug [həg]		bang [bæŋ]	— bank [bæŋk]
lung [ləŋ]	— lug [ləg]		rang [ræŋ]	— rank [ræŋk]
sang [sæŋ]	— sag [sæg]		ring [rɪŋ]	— rink [rɪŋk]
gang [gæŋ]	— gag [gæg]		thing [θɪŋ]	— think [θɪŋk]

[w]

1. Phonetic symbol and I.D. number: [w], C-21
2. Production information: a voiced, bilabial glide sound
3. Positions in words: initial and medial
4. Typical spellings: **w**ill, **o**ne, q**u**ick
5. Use as a silent letter of the alphabet: kno**w**, se**w**, sa**w**, **w**rong
6. Visible information: the lips being drawn together or puckered
7. Initial blends: [kw] quiet, choir; [tw] twin, twice; [sw] sweet, swim

[w] Word List

Initial	*Medial*
water ['wɔ tɚ]	awake [ə 'wek]
we [wi]	always ['ɔl wez]
way [we]	anyway ['ɛn i ˌwe]
went [wɛnt]	everyone ['ɛv ri ˌwən]
were [wɚ]	sandwich ['sænd wɪtʃ]

Contrasting Consonants:

[w]	[v]		[w]	[r]
went [wɛnt]	— vent [vɛnt]		wake [wek]	— rake [rek]
wine [waɪn]	— vine [vaɪn]		went [wɛnt]	— rent [rɛnt]
worse [wɚs]	— verse [vɚs]		wipe [waɪp]	— ripe [raɪp]
wail [wel]	— veil [vel]		weight [wet]	— rate [ret]
wet [wɛt]	— vet [vɛt]		ways [wez]	— rays [rez]

1. Phonetic symbol and I.D. number: [l], C-9
2. Production information: a voiced, alveolar glide sound
3. Positions in words: initial and medial
4. Typical spellings: like, hello
5. Use as a silent letter of the alphabet: calm, palm
6. Visible information: movement of tongue tip leaving the gum ridge
7. Initial blends: [bl] blame, bleed; [fl] flag, flame; [gl] glad, glue; [kl] climb, clean; [pl] play, plenty; [sl] sleep, slow

[l] Word List

Initial	Medial
live [lɪv]	believe [bɪ 'liv]
like [laɪk]	solo ['so lo]
land [lænd]	follow ['fɑl o]
letter ['lɛt ɚ]	careless ['kɛɚ lɪs]
last [læst]	yellow ['jɛl o]

Contrasting Consonants and Blends:

[l]	[r]	[l] blends	[r] blends
law [lɔ] — raw [rɔ]		flee [fli] — free [fri]	
lake [lek] — rake [rek]		cloud [klæʊd] — crowd [kræʊd]	
lace [les] — race [res]		clue [klu] — crew [kru]	
lie [laɪ] — rye [raɪ]		glass [glæs] — grass [græs]	
limb [lɪm] — rim [rɪm]		fly [flaɪ] — fry [fraɪ]	

[r]

1. Phonetic symbol and I.D. number: [r], C-14
2. Production information: a voiced, alveolar-palatal glide sound
3. Positions in words: initial and medial
4. Typical spellings: **r**ight, ca**rr**y
5. Visible information: the lips drawing together or puckering
7. Initial blends: [br] bright, broom; [dr] drink, dream; [gr] grow, great [kr] cream, cross; [pr] price, proud; [ʃr] shrink, shread; [tr] trip, trap [θr] three, thread

[r] Word List

Initial	*Medial*
road [rod]	every ['ɛv ri]
ride [raɪd]	already [ɔl 'rɛd i]
room [rum]	caress [kə 'rɛs]
wrap [ræp]	arrest [ə 'rɛst]
round [ræʊnd]	around [ə 'ræʊnd]

Contrasting Consonants:

[r]		[w]	[r]		[l]
run [rən]	—	one [wən]	erect [ə 'rɛkt]	—	elect [ə 'lɛkt]
rate [ret]	—	wait [wet]	correct [kə 'rɛkt]	—	collect [kə 'lɛkt]
rise [raɪz]	—	wise [waɪz]	berry ['bɛɚ i]	—	belly ['bɛl i]
ride [raɪd]	—	wide [waɪd]	bereaved [bɪ 'rivd]	—	believed [bɪ 'livd]
rare [rɛɚ]	—	wear [wɛɚ]	berated [bɪ 'ret ɪd]	—	belated [bɪ 'let ɪd]

[j]

1. Phonetic symbol and I.D. number: [j], C-23
2. Production information: a voiced, alveolar-palatal glide sound
3. Positions in words: initial and medial
4. Typical spellings: **y**es, on**i**on, val**ue**
5. Visible information: narrow mouth opening, relaxed lips, often revealed by context
6. Initial blends: [bju] beauty, abuse; [kju] cute, accuse; [mju] mule, amuse

[j] Word List

Initial	*Medial*
yes [jɛs]	onion ['ən jən]
year [jɪɚ]	amuse [ə 'mjuz]
your [jʊɚ]	loyal ['lɔɪ (j)əl]
you [ju]	abuse [ə 'bjuz]
yet [jɛt]	million [‚mɪl jən]

Contrasting Sounds:

[ju]	[u]	[j]	[dʒ]
feud [fjud] —	food [fud]	yam [jæm] —	jam [dʒæm]
mute [mjut] —	moot [mut]	yell [jɛl] —	jell [dʒɛl]
beauty ['bju ti] —	booty ['bu ti]	yacht [jɑt] —	jot [dʒɑt]
Butte [bjut] —	boot [but]	use [jus] —	juice [dʒus]
use [juz] —	ooze [uz]	yet [jɛt] —	jet [dʒɛt]

ABOUT THE AUTHOR

Bernard Silverstein received his doctorate from Purdue University in 1953. He served as the founding Director of the Hearing and Speech Center at the University of Tennessee from 1953 to 1966, and has been on the teaching faculty since 1953. He created and presented a daily speech improvement television series for children, from 1956 to 1964, as a public service. In addition to teaching classes in phonetics, articulation disorders, and voice disorders, he has taught many speech improvement classes for nonnative speakers of English. Since 1967, Dr. Silverstein has been a Professor in the Department of Audiology and Speech Pathology at the University of Tennessee, Knoxville.